FOR WORSE

Walking Gracefully during God's Restoration Forward

MARLISSA

ISBN Hardback: 9781087974132
ISBN Paperback: 9781088049679
ISBN eBook: 9781088049747
Subject heading: WOMEN/MARRIAGE/CHRISTIAN LIFE

For flawed, ordinary women who know that God is present and powerful in dead spaces.

Contents

Message to the Reader

I wish I could tell you that life in my Christian household is a 21st century version of the Camdens from *7th Heaven* or IG posts of prominent Bible teachers and ministry leaders, where arguments are whispered—the harshest words used are "sweetheart" and "bae." Family members pray together. They support each other. They listen to each other. They value each other. They love and respect each other. They prioritize each other. They seek God together. They walk in God's plan and purpose together. They grow together. They learn from each other. They challenge each other to be greater. It's them and God against the world.

That paragraph may read like hate, but it ain't. No Christian household is perfect, but it does not have to be dysfunctional. When you are a believer, you have the Holy Spirit. The Holy Spirit's job (these are just a few items from His resume) is to draw people to Him, cause people to seek Him, reveal spiritual truth, convict of sin, and transform us into the image of Christ (John 6:14; 14:15-17; 14:26; 16:8; and Romans 8:29). The Holy Spirit has never been written up or put on a performance plan for not doing His job. However, He will not force you, and He will go silent. Transformation is a process in which the cake is not done until we reach heaven. Oh, but it is baking daily. Similarly, we can become carnal Christians. Don't act surprised. You know, we love Jesus but do life on our own terms. My husband and I became masters at disguising the self-inflicted (our choices and decisions) dysfunction in our home.

So, my sister, you may read some words that are not so nice. There are a few curse words, sexual content, and some raggedy stuff. You may even think, *Why would she share this out loud?* Well, it was tough, but the first reason is out of obedience. God told me to write my journey; He knew who and what would be on the journey, so you are free to ask Him. Second, I have loved God most of my life and have desired to live according to His word. I have gotten a lot of stuff wrong. After years of praying for my marriage, I wanted God to "do something," and He did. So, my story is to testify of God's goodness and faithfulness for struggling people like me. Third, you can't keep moving toward God and stay the same. We have to be willing to turn the spotlight on our lives to be transformed.

Albert Einstein, a well-known theoretical physicist and agnostic, said that doing the same things and expecting different results is insanity. Perhaps that is when you have control of the results. In a walk with God, sometimes doing the same thing is good; it may take years to see different results or any results. Who's insane? God, for His process and timing, or me, for trusting His timing and process? I never used to pray for God to restore my marriage—I would say I didn't want what I had. Then I read Deuteronomy 30:2-6, where God gathered His people from all the places He'd scattered them in captivity and restored them. He prospered them, and they had more than their fathers. I will keep trusting and obeying God as long as it takes to get restored blessings.

Now, you have a little heads-up. Grab a cup of coffee, tea, or wine. Join my journey and watch God show His presence and power in dark spaces as He restores me forward.

Marlissa

For Worse

Chapter One

Living in the Middle

WHAT I do demonstrates what I believe about God. I am mustering the energy to say "yes" to God again. See, the problem is that God wants me to write this story in "the middle." I love my husband and want to be married, but we do not live or function like we are married. The middle is the space between "I do" and "I don't." I have so many thoughts. I struggle with trust in the middle. Do I trust God enough to write in the middle? Is God powerful enough to control the middle? Can I mentally and physically survive, allowing God to work in the middle? I must have faith in God and leave the outcomes to Him. God wants me to expose myself in the middle. Can you relate?

I don't get to enjoy my time with God as He orchestrates my life in private on my beautiful screened-in patio. He wants me to be transparent now. I think, *God, You have got to be kidding.* I struggle to make it each day, and God wants me to say something out loud?! I am not writing this book for the wife who finds it in her hand. I am writing for me because I do not see much help for myself anywhere. There probably is, but I feel like Elijah, who was up against Baal's 450 prophets and thought he was the *only* prophet of the Lord (1 Kings 18:22). The truth: he wasn't. In fact, God had hidden 100 prophets for their safety in a cave and provided them with bread and water (1 Kings 18:4). So, I am probably not the only wife who loves God and wants her marriage to glorify God. What may be more accurate is that few wives share their matrimonial stories while they are living in the middle.

At the moment, there is seemingly no hope for my marriage. I am not ready to articulate my circumstances. Suffice it to say, it is a Lifetime movie. This book won't even be a smooth read; it'll be disjointed and raw. But this is the journey my Father has me on. I want to write loudly and clearly that I do not understand what God is doing. Isaiah 55:8-9 says, "'For My thoughts are not your thoughts, Nor are your ways My ways,' declares the LORD. 'For *as* the heavens are higher than the earth, So are My ways higher than your ways and My thoughts than your thoughts.'" I would think that God would have immediately revived my marriage without my current circumstances. God seems to want me to continue in my situation. My head would explode trying to process God's thoughts and ways. Therefore, I am learning to say to God, "I do not have to understand, but I do trust You."

My Path to "For Worse"

Few people believe that God expects us to stay in marriages that get worse. Who would or should? Let me share that I am not a theologian. I am a believer who has to intentionally allow the Holy Spirit to reveal spiritual truths to me daily. That's the level of my expertise. I am an ordinary woman who loves God, tries to cooperate with the Holy Spirit, and keeps walking this journey every day. So, when did my wonderful marriage get worse?

I was on the path to worse before I said, "I do." First, God pressed me to not live with my husband before marriage and stop having premarital sex. We had been dating for about a year and a half at the time. My faith and relationship with God were becoming more important to me. During my prayer time, I would experience God's conviction. I wanted my then-boyfriend so badly that I did not choose obedience to God over him. I didn't trust God.

Why would my premarital behavior have such an impact on my marriage? It laid the groundwork for how I would allow or prohibit God from guiding me in my marriage. It was the impetus for my husband becoming an idol (we'll get to that later). In essence, by doing things my way, I told God, "I can't trust You to handle my relationship."

My parents had taught me God's word about premarital sex. Despite this, I became sexually active. I felt terrible that I did not have the courage to stop having sex, but I continued doing it. My then-boyfriend and I were living together, and it was uncomfortable for me. I rationalized that it was okay to live with him because we planned to get married *soon*.

Guess what? "Soon" did not come. *Well, this is an opportunity to move out. I did it, God!* I moved out! *Wait, I still gotta stop having sex? Are You really going to convict me to a level where the time with my later-to-be husband was no longer enjoyable? Seriously, God?!*

I got up enough nerve to say to him, "I do not want to have sex anymore until we get married." I got a response.

My then- boyfriend said, "Okay, I'll just get that from someone else."

I looked out the car window, trying to hold back the tears. He was so casual, like sex with me could be so easily replaced. We had sex that night and I never mentioned practicing abstinence again. I did not trust God. Instead, I started a practice of not trusting God with my relationship. I was more concerned with keeping my boyfriend then, which was critical to me losing my husband now.

God knows the end from the beginning (Isaiah 46:10). He told me before I was married not to live with my husband. I knew not to, but I did it anyway. Thirty-two years later, my husband and I are still married but live separately. God told me to stop (I knew not to start) having sex outside of marriage. Today, my husband and I are married, but he has sex with another woman.

Next, God prompted me to write my story on December 3, 2021, but I did not. I was afraid because the enemy continued to remind me of my circumstances. I maintained my devotional journal, which was kind of like being obedient, right? I was writing—just not what God told me to write. *No, Marlissa, not obedient.*

On October 20, 2022, I had a wonderful time of devotion and was convicted about my disobedience. God simple whispered, "Didn't I tell you to journal the journey?" I wanted to write. But nothing in my marriage had gotten better. I didn't know how to write that I was trusting God but that my marriage had gotten worse, so I didn't write anything at all. Again, I didn't trust God. I am Marlissa. I am learning to trust God.

Spouses have different perspectives about their marriages, and my husband is entitled to his. *Perhaps God will work things so that this becomes a joint effor*t, I thought. In my marriage, there was minimal leaving and cleaving. What does that mean? I didn't know either until I started teaching premarital counseling about ten years into my marriage. Over a span of ten years, my husband and I taught couples of all ages and levels of faith from our church who were interested in learning about marriage done the biblical way (which was not what my husband and I practiced in our marriage) using H. Norman Wright's *Before You Say "I Do"* marriage preparation study.

My husband taught about eighty percent of the content. Each week, he was compelling, charismatic, funny, and captivating. And each week, engaged couples were mesmerized by his passion for them and marriage done God's way. Heck, I was mesmerized by my husband each week until the day after the premarital counseling session when I thought, *Wait, we don't accept each other's uniqueness. We don't have a vision statement. We don't make fulfilling each other's needs a priority. Our roles and responsibilities were established by default, not through discussion. That's not how we handle conflict, manage finances, govern in-laws, prepare for sex, or nurture our spiritual intimacy as a couple.*

I started resenting my husband because I wondered what was wrong with me that he wasn't to me what he taught to the couples in our class. That was it for me in a nutshell. I stopped teaching my twenty percent of the course content and just enjoyed the couples' fellowship. My husband's life was full, and I was trying to find space in it. I did what all two-year-olds do when they don't get their way: I acted out.

As I reflect on things, I realize there was a leave-and-cleave problem early in our marriage. One, we had false practices before we were married, so I was fighting to be seen by my husband as his human priority, not an afterthought. Nothing changed from the Friday before our wedding to our wedding day to the day after. We had functioned under the pretense of a covenant relationship and never transitioned to a covenant marriage.

One day when we were arguing and my husband was about to leave, I became desperate to get him to stay. I pretended that I was going to take a bottle of Tylenol pills. Let's just say that I did not get the results I expected. Calling 911 is serious (as it should be). I spent a week on the psychiatric floor of a local hospital. (This was not a healthy way to try to get attention!) Of course, I did not get my husband's attention. In fact, it was over twenty-five years later before we mentioned the incident again. Still, he could not understand that all I wanted was him.

My husband and I kept living life. Living developed into cycles of toxic behaviors (yeah, more on that later). I was praying fervently for me, my husband, and my marriage. I desperately wanted a marriage that glorified God. However, I did not trust God to do it. I became . . . well, let's just say, as I have been told, "a terrible wife, disrespectful, and evil." This is probably the only description suitable for a Bible study setting. The thing is, I loved (and still love) my husband. Unfortunately, I seemed to get blamed for most things in my marriage, so I began to take ownership for its demise. I shouldered that it became ruined because of all the things I said and did (yeah, more on that later).

That's how I got to *For Worse*. You know, the part of the wedding vows that talks about loving, honoring, and cherishing for better or worse? That's where I am. What do I do? Have you recovered from "for worse"? I don't know how you got to the space that seems like there is no return in your marriage. There is much material on how not to get there. But what if you didn't understand clearly that it was where you were headed? Or perhaps you sensed it, but neither you nor your spouse were willing to do the things necessary to keep your marriage from getting to "for worse."

I prayed desperately for my marriage. I have over thirteen years of my prayers pouring out to God. That was when I started maintaining my prayers digitally. My outcry to God started more than twenty years ago. Why wouldn't the God who loves me and ordained marriage not respond to my prayers for a marriage that would glorify Him? I didn't know. I still don't know.

Now that I have gotten myself into this "for worse" space, is there any hope for me? I could not find any resurrecting power marital stories to be encouraged by. I am sure they exist, but I could not find them. I encountered stories about how not to get to "for worse" and how God forgives divorce. But what about *this* space? There is this dreaded space in the middle that no one wants to get to and apparently God may not have presence (He's not there) or power (He can't do anything in it). It's the space where we grab His hand again after going through divorce. Wait. That can't be right. That can't be how God works. Oh, right, we pacify ourselves in this space. We say to our spouse, "I married the wrong person. I can't live with you. I have no peace with you. You don't make me a priority. God has something better for me. God doesn't want me to live like this. I can't please you. I have lost who I am. You are disrespectful. You are contentious. You are evil. You aren't nice to me. You don't satisfy me. I am not happy. We have grown apart. You were only for a season. I have met someone else and blah, blah, blah, blah." What does *any* of this have to do with what *God* says about marriage?

Remember, I am not Minister Marlissa; I am an ordinary woman who loves God and is trying to live according to His plan and purpose. But all the excuses I mentioned sound like some bull. They sound like husbands and wives who want to live according to their own plans and not surrender to the word of God. So, fellow believer in Christ, what do you believe about God? Is the space you are currently in too difficult for God? Is He just conveniently silent? This is a real "we" situation, not a me-trying-to-connect-with-you circumstance. I, just like you, must decide what I will believe.

In my "for worse" space, I wonder, *Do I really want to trust God for my marriage? I might have to surrender and allow God to transform me. Wait, transform me? What about what my husband said and did?* Fellow sister in Christ, we have allowed the world to tell us that both spouses have to want the marriage to work. When did God need to tap someone in to help Him? God, who established and ordained marriage, can't maintain it? Is there a space where God does not reign? *Can I trust God's process and timing however He decides to work and however long it takes? Yikes! Do I believe marriage is God's idea?* Remember, I am no biblical scholar. I am just crazy enough to take God at His word.

God-Established Marriage

"And the LORD God fashioned into a woman the rib which He had taken from the man, and brought her to the man. The man said, 'At last this is bone of my bones, And flesh of my flesh;

She shall be called 'woman,' Because she was taken out of man.' For this reason a man shall leave his father and his mother, and be joined to his wife; and they shall become one flesh" (Genesis 2:22–24).

"And said, 'For this reason a man shall leave his father and mother and be joined to his wife, and the two shall become one flesh'? So they are no longer two, but one flesh. Therefore, what God has joined together, no person is to separate" (Matthew 19:5–6).

"'For this reason a man shall leave his father and mother, and the two shall become one flesh; so they are no longer two, but one flesh. Therefore, God has joined together, no person is to separate'" (Mark 10:7–9).

"For this reason a man shall leave his father and his mother and be joined to his wife, and the two shall become one flesh" (Ephesians 5:31).

Our Omnipresent Heavenly Father

"'Am I a God who is near,' declares the Lord, 'And not a God far off? Can a man hide himself in hiding places. So I do not see him?' declares the Lord. 'Do I not fill the heavens and the earth?' declares the LORD" (Jeremiah 23:23–24).

Nothing Is Too Hard for God

"For nothing will be impossible with God" (Luke 1:37).

"'Behold, I am the LORD, the God of all flesh; is anything too difficult for Me?'" (Jeremiah 32:27).

"'I know that You can *do* all things'"
(Job 42:2).

I don't know how to cross-check biblical texts and contextualize everything (you do not need to be a Bible scholar to trust God). I know my Father said He is a present help. He said He cares about me. He said He would never leave me nor forsake me. Therefore, I am willing to trust that God is with me in this "for worse" season of my life.

The Message and Instructions

On December 3, 2021, God shared a message and instructions during my time of devotion and my plea for my marriage. By this point, my marriage was dead. My husband still stayed in our home but lived in the upstairs loft. We had not been intimate since October of 2021 and had very limited conversations. God shared with me that He would, in fact, resurrect and restore my marriage. God said that we would return to the premarital counseling ministry He called us to. He would handle my spouse, and I was to journal the journey. He gave me two passages of Scripture: Daniel 3:16-18 and Ezekiel 37:3-8.

In the Book of Daniel chapter three, King Nebuchadnezzar had given a decree that every person should bow down and worship a golden image he'd had made when a certain type of music was played. Those who defied the decree would be tossed into a fiery furnace. Three Jewish boys did not comply to the decree, so they were brought before the king to answer for their defiance. The three Jewish boys did not see a need to defend themselves to the king because their defiance of the king's decree was because of their obedience to God. Further, they believed assuredly that God could deliver them from the consequence (being thrown into the fiery furnace) for disobeying the decree. Even if God decided not to deliver them, they would still not disobey God by worshiping the golden image (Daniel 3:1-30). Like the three Jewish boys, I have come to understand that I do not have to defend God or my trust in Him. If God does not do what He said to me about restoring my marriage, He still loves me (and I still love Him). I finally have the faith and courage to write that statement.

God also shared Ezekiel 37:3-8 with me. In this passage, the prophet Ezekiel describes a valley of dry bones. It was a place of death and hopelessness. God told Ezekiel that He could cause the dead bones to come back to life. Then, Ezekiel spoke to the bones, and they began to come together. The bones knew how to connect to each other. They were covered with flesh and skin, but they still didn't have life. The bones needed God's spirit for them to come to life. Once God's breath entered them, they came to life, stood up, and became an exceedingly great army. This story reminded me that God is both present and powerful in dead spaces.

The type of message God gave me about my marriage was not new to me. He had given me radical faith messages before. At four months old, my eldest daughter developed cardiomyopathy. One day in February 1996, my husband and I were told that she would probably not make it through the night. But she made it through the night. The only option to save her was a heart transplant. The doctors said if she could make it to May, she could probably receive a heart from organ donors who got into accidents over Memorial Day weekend. Yeah, those words actually came out of one of their mouths.

As much as I wanted my daughter to live, I could not fathom another mother going through what I was going through. I prayed and was convinced that God would heal my daughter without a transplant. Please don't get me wrong, I am not opposed to organ donation. I am an organ donor. However, I was convinced that a heart transplant was not how God would come through in my daughter's case. We stood on God's word, and just as quickly as the condition developed, it left eight years later. For eight years, nothing changed. We kept believing and living out radical faith.

It somehow seems that God likes to stretch me in exercising radical faith when it comes to my children. My second daughter had a bone marrow transplant to cure sickle cell disease when she was fourteen years old. None of our family members were a marrow donation match.

Therefore, she had to have an unrelated donor, which has a higher mortality rate. Again, God shared that He would heal my daughter. My family and I believed, and God did exactly what He said He would do. She was healed of sickle cell disease through the bone marrow transplant.

So, why was the message from God about my marriage so difficult for me to grasp? I don't know if my stories made you say, "Wow!" or not. There are many moms who have radical faith stories about their children. Most of us would never give up praying for our children. Why couldn't I grasp this message about my marriage like there was no other option? (Ahh, that's it!) When it comes to marriage, we have other options. We don't have to burden ourselves with sacrificial prayers or radical faith.

I was scared to start writing this book. What if God didn't resurrect my marriage? Today, almost a year and a half later, He still hasn't. In fact, it has gotten worse. It's not funny, but "for worse" has gotten worser! But I finally decided to be obedient and write anyway. Priscilla Shirer often says that God speaks to be obeyed, not heard.

Living Life

My husband and I put our house on the market in January of 2022 I said, "God, it is the wrong direction." We took the house off the market in February so that my husband could move to an apartment. Again, I said, "God, it is the wrong direction." I thought, *Ok, God, You've got this. Maybe You need to get us alone so that You can work on my husband?* Since *I* wanted my marriage, *I* didn't need much work, right? I started enjoying having time for myself. God was handling my husband, and things would get back to normal. (Hold up!) "Normal" was actually the problem.

Remember the cycles of toxic behavior I mentioned? My husband and I would separate, then just come back together. Like the dry bones I mentioned in Ezekiel 37:3-8, we had sinews, flesh, and skin each time, but there was no breath in us. While I was thinking my husband was the only one who needed to be worked on, I didn't accept that God had to transform both of us to give us new life. We needed the breath of the Holy Spirit in our marriage.

Everything sounded good, but I did not trust God enough to write this book. I didn't think I needed much transformation and was hands-off with my husband. I prayed for him daily, as usual, but I let God do God. My husband self-declared that he was no longer married, and I awaited divorce papers. *Why hadn't God given him the same message and instructions? Had I misheard since I seemed to be the only one with the message?* Instead of trusting God, I needed my husband's voice to validate God's voice. I waited and waited, but the divorce papers did not come.

After a couple of months of not being around one another, my husband and I saw each other in May. I recall telling my girlfriend (who is walking this journey with me) and writing in my journal that my husband still loved me. God was working. I still was disobedient in writing the book God told me to write—lackluster in my desire for transformation and discouraged because I was the only one with the message.

Time continued to pass with us having minimal contact, then God revealed to me in a dream that my husband had a girlfriend. In the dream, I said to a woman, "Are you dating my husband?" Two days later, I saw a picture in the family group chat of my husband with a woman who would later become his girlfriend. (I told you this was a Lifetime movie.) Today, I don't understand, but I trust God. I said, "God, what the . . .? I thought You said You would handle him. This ain't handling him at all. Wrooong direction, God."

A few weeks later, I saw an event on my calendar for a trip to San Francisco in October. I clicked on the event and the picture for the event was of my husband and the same woman who was in the photo from my family group chat. The woman sent the event request, so I was able to see her email address. Prior to this moment, my husband's events had never shown up on my calendar before. When I told my husband that his trip with a woman was on my calendar, he responded, "Which woman?" Incidentally, I emailed the woman to let her know—in case she did not know—that the man she was dating was legally married and had not filed for divorce. I asked her to step away until we were divorced. I told her that my marriage journey would be a testimony and that she could choose how she would be represented. See, when my husband and I thought we could try to be one flesh and act "married" before we were by living together, it was easy to think we could just leave and declare ourselves "unmarried."

Blindsided

One of my favorite movies is *The Blind Side*, which is about the life of football player Micheal Oher. Blindside is a football position in which the offensive lineman protects the quarterback's area that is difficult for him to see. I experienced the ultimate blindside when I discovered my husband had a girlfriend. I did not think he could do that, not so much because of me but because of his relationship with God. Interestingly, I had a dream two nights before the morning I found out about his girlfriend.

I was devastated and broken. All this time, I thought God had been working things out. I thought, *Now this?! We were already struggling, then he added a layer of ultimate betrayal.* I did not get it. *Why wouldn't he just file for divorce if he was going to start dating?* I thought.

Well, it took me months to understand that God did not blindside me. God is and has always been in control. He gets to decide how and when things happen. Although this part of the journey was painful for me, God was and is a present help. It was an opportunity to trust God regardless of what was going on around me.

God has healed my heart and continues to heal it (more about that shortly). I am still trusting God. Is God really going to resurrect my marriage? I still don't know, but I would rather trust Him than not.

One morning, I woke up thinking, *God, this is tough. You got me out here raggedy in front of anyone reading this book. You know the realness of my circumstances.* God reminded me of the passage in John 11:39-42 when Jesus was speaking with Martha several days after the death of her brother, Lazarus. First, Jesus said to her, "Remove the stone," when she said that his body had a stench since her brother had been dead for four days (John 11:39). God told me that He needs my marriage to smell really bad to the point where most of what my husband sees in me is evil, disrespectful, and contentious and most of what I see in him is cowardice and betrayal. It's about getting our relationship to a point where sin is no longer sin, a call is no longer a calling, a covenant is no longer a covenant, Jesus is no longer the model, and God's word is no longer valid. Just as Jesus continues His conversation with Martha, I believe I will see the glory of God, and everyone who reads this testimony will know that Jesus is who He says He is.

You do not need a special message from God to believe Him to guide you to a marriage that is restored forward. A marriage that glorifies Him is His will for everyone. I don't think that you have to fight for your marriage. I believe you have to make a decision to surrender and trust Him.

Now that you know a little more about my story, the rest is an amazing journey of love and intimacy with my Father. The worst time in my life is the best time of my life.

Restoration Forward

What is your story? Are there parts of your story that you just cannot say out loud yet? Has God placed a specific verse on your heart to hold to? Do you think God can do the impossible?

_____

_____

_____

_____

_____

_____

_____

_____

_____

_____

_____

_____

_____

_____

_____

_____

_____

_____

_____

_____

For Worse

Chapter Two

Finding My Fabulous Four

DO you believe that God cares about the details of your life? I have never really needed people to help me "do life." I prayed for people pretty often, but I rarely asked them to pray for me. I seldom shared the details of my life. In my social circles, since I was a minister's wife, I provided godly insight.

Deneka, a longtime college friend, had been walking the marital journey with me for several months before my husband moved out. Do you have college buddies who know just enough about you and will ensure that some information will go to the grave? That's Deneka. During late 2021, our relationship became more spiritual; she became a source of support and accountability. I started to become more and more transparent with her, and she constantly strengthened me with God's word and prayers over me.

God knew I would need even more support than Deneka, so He sent me even more help. I had been experiencing a brokenness I could not have imagined. My body ached. I lost my appetite. I could not sleep, and I feared going out of the house. When I left the house, I had panic attacks. I was a complete mess. I was angry with God, but I needed Him. I had started attending a different church from the one where my husband and I were members a few months earlier and contemplated reaching out to a lady I met at a ministry outing. Deneka had a demanding job, so I did not want to keep contacting her during the day. But I needed help. I thought, *God, should I text this lady and ask her to partner with me in prayer regarding my marriage?* Silence.

While I was eating my lunch one day, I asked, "God, who can I ask to partner with me in prayer for my marriage?"

He said, "Donna."

I replied, "Donna who?"

He told me her last name.

I knew of Donna from the church where I had attended and my husband was on staff, but we were not friends. And I certainly was not prepared to partner with someone in my husband's circle. Out of obedience, I apprehensively texted Donna, and she agreed to meet with me the next day. We talked for close to four hours. I felt so free to share with her.

When I finished sharing, she quickly and enthusiastically said, "You are my assignment." Just like that, she joined my marital journey. Donna said I needed to know that I was God's beloved daughter (whenever she addresses me, she calls me "Beloved"). She had only moved to my area about a week earlier. She later told me that she believed I was part of why God moved her and her husband south.

In addition to Deneka and Donna, God brought two other ladies along my journey; I call them my "Fabulous Four." God handcrafted a team for me. Again, I have never had these kinds of relationships before. God knew exactly what I needed and provided it for me. He knew the work He was about to do in my life and gave me everything I needed. Read this loud and clear: You cannot walk this journey alone. You cannot. Don't even try it.

God will send you exactly who you need. For instance, shortly after the Fabulous Four convened in the summer of 2022, my husband wanted my daughters to spend time with him and his girlfriend. This was received differently by our three daughters; the situation wreaked havoc on me and my girls. My husband said that his actions as a husband had nothing to do with him being a father. (I do not know how true that is.) What I knew was my daughters and I were impacted by him having a wife *and* a girlfriend. He was adamant that he wanted to be divorced, yet he still had not filed the papers. I knew what God had told me, but my pain was unbearable; I was trying to do damage control with my daughters.

Eventually, I filed for divorce in September 2022. I was expecting my husband to sign the acknowledgement of receipt of the papers the moment he received them. I planned a brunch for the Fabulous Four in early October 2022 to meet each other and be with me for support because I expected the divorce to be finalized or close to finalized by then. I was trying to enjoy planning the brunch and not focus on the fact that it would also mark the end of my marriage, but at the end of September, my husband called me and said that he couldn't sign the papers because he was still in love with me. However, he said he couldn't live with me. For the next several months, my husband and I entered into these cycles of "I love you," "you have my heart," "I can't live with you," "I can end it with her at any time," "I want someone to feed me, f—k me, and fellowship with me. I have that with her," "you are evil and disrespectful," "I have no future with her," "I have peace," and "God's plan will stand."

My Fabulous Four, especially Donna and Deneka, walked with me through all of this. I thought I was on a marital journey. All of what I had gone through and continue to go through has been worth it because of my spiritual bond with Donna and Deneka. I have been searching for words, but I literally cannot find any that give justice to how thankful and appreciative I am to them. At my worst, they were there. I am overwhelmed as I write this book because God showed me how much He loves me by using them to speak to me in my situation. For me, they modeled how God would love me if He were a human walking with me today. It was like I had God's comfort through them. Sometimes, I texted Donna from such a place of pain, then the next thing I knew, she was at my door. She and Deneka let me experience hurt in my own way but consistently pointed me to God and His word. I am good at being sarcastic and cynical when I am angry or hurt. I sometimes lashed out because they always took God's perspective (which was consistent with His word) and held me accountable. They loved me.

Turn off the Life Support

I had a few days of insanity in January 2023. I was having a difficult time, so I decided that the very folks God selected to walk with me on this journey were too much for me. Too much love, too much truth, too much compassion, too much faith, too much accountability—just too much. So, with my limited wisdom, I sent a text to Donna, Deneka, and another woman in the Fabulous Four saying, "I need a break from you all. Please don't reach out." (Yeah, I did that.)

For three days, I went without lifesaving medication in the form of the support these women had been giving me. By the end of the first day, I desperately wanted one of them to reach out. I was certain they were praying for me, but I also knew they would allow the Holy Spirit to work out what was needed without interference. By the afternoon of the third day, my pride had been whipped out of me. I reached out. And just like that, they received me back. Now, in love and fun, they remind me of when I tried to "drop" them. I share this because I am just like you—making mistakes but committed to cooperating with the Holy Spirit to be transformed into the image of Jesus!

Most mornings, Donna would send a text first thing saying, "This is your word for today," then share with me whatever she believed God wanted me to know. Her texts also included a link to a praise and worship song. Almost every time, what she sent addressed the very thing I had prayed about or had been struggling with the night before. I am telling you, I am an ordinary woman of God, yet God worked behind the scenes of life and orchestrated these people to be in my life. This is what authentic Christian relationships look like.

One time, I was having a really difficult time, and I literally had been calling on the name of Jesus for several hours during the night. Finding no relief, I texted my Fabulous Four, not expecting a response at that time. But Donna responded. She did what she does and responded with encouraging and uplifting words. I wasn't hearing it, though. I went on a rant about how I had been calling on the name of Jesus and He didn't help me and blah, blah, blah. She politely responded, "God did hear you and is helping you. He woke me up so that I could talk with you." (Drop the mic.)

Donna, Deneka, and I have long, wonderful talks about anything and everything, but our conversations always get us back to God's goodness. You must have people who love you enough to say what needs to be said but will also stay with you as you move forward. Donna and Deneka highlighted my anxiety, pride, self-pity, and lack of self-control (hmmm, my cycle of rants) during our discussions. I did not want to hear what they had to say, but I needed to hear it. They walked with me as we prayed for the Holy Spirit to transform me. They were sensitive to the Holy Spirit in things I needed to be convicted of, didn't co-sign mess, and walked with me. And they did this day in and day out.

One thing I especially loved about our relationship during that time was that Donna and Deneka asked tough questions. I can often have two text conversations with Donna and Deneka about the same thing, and it is almost as if they are copying and pasting their responses. Nearly every single time, the Holy Spirit spoke a consistent message to them to share with me. I recall being asked, "Marlissa, did you walk away from your calling?" I thought, *What?* I always viewed leaving the premarital counseling ministry as my husband and me not living what we were teaching, which gave me the right to stop. (Didn't it?) This question forced me to have a conversation with God. I concluded that God had not uncalled us. I don't know how often I was asked, "Is God sovereign or not?" It forced me to affirm out loud that He is.

Donna suggested that I take a trip during the Christmas holiday of 2022. I contemplated traveling alone, but then I asked God who I should travel with. He said I should go with Deneka. When I asked her, she immediately said "yes." Two weeks later, she asked where we were going. (She responded "yes" to a ten-day trip without knowing where she was going.) I had never taken a girls' trip before, but it was an unforgettable ten-day cruise. I called it the "Greater Cruise" because Deneka and I experienced God and each other at a whole new level.

God did not mean for us to go through life alone. There are people that God can bring into your life who will love you genuinely and allow you to be transparent. They will sharpen and challenge you to be transformed into the image of Jesus. It took me a lifetime and this "for worse" season to experience these relationships. None of my Fabulous Four ladies knew each other before I introduced them. However, Donna and Deneka have developed their own relationship outside of my marital journey and support each other. Deneka, Donna, and I also formed Naomi's Club, where we are committed to praying for our adult daughters.

During this time on my journey, I also sought the help of a medical professional and selected a therapist with a Christian practice. I spent about ten weeks in therapy. It was helpful but was secondary to the specific support God had given me. Additionally, God impressed upon me to reach out to a family friend who is a pastor. Confidentially, I asked him to pray for me and my husband. A spiritual community is critical for prayer, counsel, contemplation of God's word, and fellowship; reciprocal relationships are formed in community. God has equipped us to both give and receive from each other.

One area of support in which I continue to seek God for is my church community. I stopped attending the church where I was a member and my husband served on staff. In late summer of 2022, I watched my husband preach a sermon online around Psalm 51 about David and his adultery. The sermon was solid scripturally, and my husband is gifted with his voice and delivery. I could not wait until the sermon was over because I thought, *Surely preparing this anointed word would bring him to repentance.* (It did not.)

I mentioned the incident to my therapist, and she strongly suggested that I contact the pastor. At the time, I did not want to do that. My therapist said that the pastor had a right to know for the sake of the sanctity of the pulpit and to provide my husband with the appropriate discipleship. She suggested that I send a letter anonymously since I did not feel comfortable talking to the pastor. In October 2022, I sent the pastor an anonymous letter indicating that my husband was having a public affair, and I revealed the name of his girlfriend.

After a prompting from the Holy Spirit, I recently shared with the pastor that I sent the anonymous letter and that it is difficult for women who are married to leaders in the church to get support. The meeting went well, and I appreciated the insight and care the pastor provided.

I continue to visit churches, but it is difficult. When I disclose my marital status, "men of the church" say things like, "invite him [my husband] to our men's group" and "he just needs to be around some strong godly men." I chuckle and think, *Yeah, my husband's that strong godly man at his church. No, thank you.*

Words from the Fabulous Four Spoken over Me

Donna's View

"This woman . . . God's beloved daughter . . . appointed and anointed for such a time as this . . . Chosen among women . . . Set aside for God's glory . . . hidden beneath the shroud of performance, perfection, and priorities . . . now revealed, uncovered . . . a precious jewel discovered . . . finally."

"She has no idea . . . the impact that she's had on my life, my faith, and my obedience to our Father. My trust has been renewed by her faith, her doubts, and her fears. I trust God on a whole new level—daily faith, moment-by-moment—child-like trust in the Almighty God in every area of my life. I believe in the impossible, the unlikely, and the uncommon."

"A surrendered life being pursued by God at all costs. Beloved, I love you."

Deneka's View

As I sit here taking in the sun, sky, breeze, and all the natural creations by God, I reflect on this past year and the journey with my sister, Marlissa. She has asked me to be part of her story and write about it as the Holy Spirit leads. Here goes.

I have known Marlissa since my freshman year of college. We became sorority sisters—sisters for life. Our lives took different directions the years after undergrad. However, whenever we linked up once per year, it was always as though we never lost touch. Our relationship went to a new level of friendship and sisterhood in 2021. Why this year? Marlissa's journey took her in a direction that I know she never anticipated. Although this included some challenges and difficulties in her marriage, God showed His mercy, grace, and awesome Holy Spirit in ways none of us could have imagined. She and I have had the best spiritual encounters just talking about our life experiences and everything that has brought us to this point in our lives.

I am not a person to share my business, not even to mention my emotional side. I lock most thoughts and feelings deeply in a nicely decorated box. That is me. Decorated, calm, cool, and always collected. Well, the inside struggles with many thoughts of pessimism, hopelessness, and some brokenness. This year had been the exception, where God showed up so many times to remind me that He is still with me; I am His daughter.

Marlissa had no idea how God used her, even in her most hurtful times, to show that He will direct our paths when we acknowledge Him in all things. Oh, and one of my favorite reminders is that all things work together for the good of those who love God and are called according to His good purpose (Romans 8:28).

My prayer life has been restored; there have been so many unexpected times that God would move me to pray for Marlissa and her situation. I left my prayer life a while ago. I let the enemy whisper to me that I was not worthy or "clean" enough for God to use me to pray for someone else. Even as I write this, the tears flow. They are not tears of sadness but humility and gratitude over the fact that God loves us despite ourselves and what the enemy tries to say to us. The Holy Spirit takes over, and the prayer language is prevalent. I love experiencing oneness with God the Father, the Son, and the Holy Spirit! I love surrendering to allow the Holy Spirit to pray for what is needed, especially when I am lost in my thoughts.

Marlissa and I took a ten-day cruise last year, and we had the most awesome time just watching God in nature and being vulnerable. I have learned that God truly dwells in our vulnerability. This happens when surrender happens. At least for me, it does. I learned in one of our most casual conversations about God's healing powers that I still carried a few overnight bags (not full baggage) from two failed marriages. I actually thought it was too late for me to experience a good marriage. I am still not married. But—a huge *but*—I am no longer in bondage with thoughts that I am not worthy of marriage.

My relationship with my adult daughters has taken an unexpected turn in seeing how God truly heals, restores, and grants renewal. This is partly due to my increased prayer time and faith. Yes, all these eternal blessings came when I was lost, confused, and in bondage of doubt, uneasiness, awkwardness, and just plain old fear of the unknown. Who would have guessed that God would use Marlissa's hurt, tears, frustration, confused thoughts, and questioning of God to show His will, mercy, and grace in my life? I always tell her she is my shero and Abrahamette of faith.

I am so thankful to be on this journey with her! I am even more grateful to our Heavenly Father that His will and purpose in and for my life is manifesting right before my eyes.

Restoration Forward

Has God given you a fabulous person (or four!) to walk this journey with you? Are you willing to seek Him until He does?

_____

_____

_____

_____

_____

_____

_____

_____
_____
_____
_____
_____
_____
_____
_____
_____
_____
_____
_____
_____
_____
_____
_____
_____
_____
_____
_____
_____
_____
_____
_____
_____
_____
_____
_____
_____
_____

Finding My Fabulous Four

_____

_____

_____

_____

_____

_____

_____

_____

_____

_____

_____

_____

For Worse

.

Chapter Three

Time with My Father

FOR most of my adult life, I have been managing my family and involved in their lives at every level. I always enjoyed spending time with my Heavenly Father. Mary and Martha are sisters who had a special relationship with Jesus; however, they demonstrated their love for Him differently. I was Martha, loving God yet busy with life. My daughters' health concerns caused me to stop working when they were younger. However, God allowed me to maintain a small business that contributed to the household income and provided the appropriate caregiving for my girls. God has so orchestrated my life that I am now Mary, having the time to sit at His feet.

One of the things Donna shared with me early on was, "Marlissa, God is seeking you. Not you as a wife, mother, daughter, professor—just Marlissa." I did not understand what she meant until recently. It was difficult to comprehend that the God of the universe has all the time in the world just for me. He also has time just for you.

In recent months, Deneka shared with me that I have been waiting for my husband to walk with me in the ministry God wants me to join Him in. It is almost as if I am waiting for my husband to validate my calling. "Start walking," she said. "Your husband will join you." Deneka's words helped me to finally start writing this book. Once I started writing, I knew that I still had a level of fear. Currently, I am not writing with the boldness that you have experienced with other Bible study writers. (Remember, I am not a Bible scholar.) I am trying, with every fiber of my being, to just be obedient and trust God.

Romans 8:26–27 states, "Now in the same way the Spirit also helps our weakness; for we do not know what to pray as we should, but the Spirit Himself intercedes for *us* with groanings too deep for words; and He who searches the hearts knows what the mind of the Spirit is, because He intercedes for the saints according to *the will of* God." This verse resonates with me because it shows that God loves me so much that He provides the Holy Spirit for me and to pray for me. The Spirit guides me in not just praying for myself but in praying according to God's will for me.

I had many days when I could not pray. I could not utter a word to my Father, who was allowing painful things to happen to me. I was so conflicted. I knew I needed Him, and I wanted the relief that I knew only He could provide. But I also felt that He was the source of my pain. There were days when I literally could only say, "Help me, Jesus." On other days, I sat in my sunroom with tears in my eyes, no words. Whether it was saying "help me, Jesus" or shedding tears, the Holy Spirit took my pain and supplication and adjusted it to speak to God on my behalf according to God's perfect plan for me.

Throughout my marital journey, I've come to know that Jesus prays for me: "Who is the one who condemns? Christ Jesus is He who died, but rather, was raised, who is at the right hand of God, who also intercedes for us" (Romans 8:34). The Holy Spirit and Jesus pray for me. Do you know what that means? I didn't at the time. I did not understand that God loves me so much that He had already prepared the Holy Spirit and Jesus to be Johnny-on-the-spot when I needed intercession. While I was angry, frustrated, and a few other choice words with God, He was listening to the Holy Spirit and Jesus talk about me!

I continued to sit in His presence. I needed God to help me with my pain. I did not want to be consumed or defined by my pain. My Father led me to the book *Healing the Soul of a Woman* by Joyce Meyer. What a powerful read! I could not put it down. I did not know I could use God's word to heal my heart. What a freaking revelation! She started the book with Psalm 147:3, which says, "He heals the brokenhearted and binds up their wounds." God says that He will heal the pain and comfort the sorrow of all those whose hearts hurt. That was a promise I was willing to take hold of. There were twenty-three word-filled chapters leading to a victorious, healed heart. I was no longer in a state of sadness. My value was defined in God, not my husband or marriage. I believed what God said about me. It was okay for me to be Marlissa. I thanked God for speaking to me through Joyce Meyer's book. Today, I am thankful that my heart is healed.

During my times with my Father, I practiced a strategy suggested by my therapist on how to unhear my husband's voice. She asked me to combat every lie with God's truth. I had to be intentional whenever I replayed the hurtful things that took place in my marriage. My niece, who is a Bible study writer, gave me the book *Your Greater is Coming* by Joel Osteen to celebrate my Greater Cruise. Chapter twelve of the book is titled "Manasseh is Coming" and reveals why Joseph named his firstborn son Manasseh: "'For,' *he said,* 'God has made me forget all my trouble and all of my father's household'" (Genesis 41:51). Osteen made the connection that Joseph mentioned to his "father's household" as a way of referring to his past. *What?! God can cause me to forget my past—what was said and done to me? I'll take forgetting and unhearing for $100, please.* From that moment on, I believed God to cause me to forget what was said and done to me, and He did! Today, my heart is healed, and I have forgotten what has been said and done to me.

Don't let the enemy try to convince you that your heart being healed, forgetting, and unhearing can't happen—that you must be fooling yourself. Just because someone has not experienced it does not mean it's not real. I am a witness (and many others are too) that God does heal hearts and can cause you to forget. If someone has a problem with that, they have a problem with God. I was once told that I would become like the woman with the issue of blood, who was only known by her problem. Quite the contrary, the woman with the issue of blood is far more known for her faith in touching the hem of Jesus' garment than her blood disease (Mark 5:25-34). I decided to keep pressing until I touched His garment.

I never knew I could have deep intimacy with my Father. He loves me perfectly and wants me to depend on Him totally. He never gets tired of spending time with me. If you already know this, I hope you are having an "amen moment." If you did not know this, I hope you decide to take hold of how much God loves you and how rich it is to sit at His feet. Initially, I was sad that I had so much time on my hands. Now when I am walking by the lake, sitting in my sunroom, sitting on my patio, walking in the neighborhood, or drinking a cup of coffee talking with my Father, I say, "God, where did the time go?"

Restoration Forward

Are you comfortable with having devotional time with your Father? What does your time entail? Do you and God have special places? Consider writing a psalm to your Father (see my example).

Marlissa's Psalm

I long to spend eternity with You. Each day I have breath, I know that You have a will, plan, and purpose for me that glorifies You and contributes to Your kingdom on earth. My heart watches for the new day because You give me new loving-kindness, mercy, compassion, grace, forgiveness, power, and strength. All that I need for a life surrendered to You- You so graciously and lovingly provide. My earthly father was a loyal provider and protector. How much more is my Heavenly Father a refuge and shield for me?

I love to see Your awesomeness and greatness in creation—the sunrises and sunsets, the waves on the ocean, the wind blowing the trees, the birds flying, the smell of flowers and fresh cut grass. In all of Your vastness, You care about me. I mean, really care about me. Every detail of my life is important to You! Because of Your Sovereignty, I hope in You. I hope in Your word, and I hope in Your name.

As I walk in the golden years of life, I am thankful for Your goodness and Your mercy. Holy Spirit, teach me to follow You. May I find unspeakable joy in transforming intimacy with my Father. Greater days, My Father. Greater days.

_____

_____

_____

_____

_____

_____

_____

_____

_____

_____

_____

_____

_____

_____

_____

_____

_____

_____

_____

_____

_____

_____

_____

_____

_____

_____

_____
_____
_____
_____
_____
_____
_____
_____
_____
_____
_____
_____
_____
_____
_____
_____
_____
_____
_____
_____
_____
_____
_____

Chapter Four

I Give

THE more time I spend with my Father, the more I realize that a love relationship is a daily walk. It is not a one-and-done experience. I have a spot at a creek in my neighborhood where I go to spend time with God. The first time I went to it was at Donna's suggestion. I was distracted while doing my devotional time for a couple of days, and she said, "Go somewhere new; go to Line Creek." I grabbed a lawn chair and headed that way.

When I got to Line Creek, it was very isolated with only a couple of cars in the gravel parking lot. It had rained during the early morning, so the ground was damp. There were a couple of different trails to take, so I randomly picked one. I started walking in a secluded wooded area and became nervous thinking, *Am I going to be able to find my way back?* I checked my phone to make sure I still had cell signal. (I did.) I chuckled a little because if I had watched this as a movie, I would've thought, *Why would she go further in the woods?* I nervously kept going. Then I started to hear the sound of water. The trail transitioned from dirt to stone. The sound of water got louder, and I picked up my pace, almost running. Then I saw it: a beautiful creek. I sat at the edge and saw my God all over the place.

I had been meditating on Psalm 18, so I took out my phone to read the chapter. Then, God told me to pray for my husband's girlfriend. *No, No, No, No, No. Really, God? You expect me to pray for her?* For some reason, I never had any ill feelings or malice toward her. I knew God loved her just as much as He loved me. I knew He was pursuing her just as much as He was pursuing me. So, since He allowed her on this journey, He would also transform her. From that day forward, I prayed the same prayer for myself, my husband, and his girlfriend.

What I know is that God's will always prevails. That's not what I think; it's what His word says. I know God gives us free will and allows us to exercise it. However, that's not my problem or responsibility. God draws His beloved to Himself. Me, you, my husband, and his girlfriend are God's beloved.

God's Plan Will Go Forth

"'I know that You can *do* all things,
And that no plan is impossible for You'"
(Job 42:2).

"For it is God who is at work in you,
both to desire and to work for *His* good
pleasure" (Philippians 2:13).

"For those whom He foreknew, He
also predestined *to become* conformed to
the image of His Son, so that He would be
the firstborn among many *brothers and
sisters*" (Romans 8:29).

I decided to be obedient. God had something good
and perfect for my husband's girlfriend; I knew it was not
my husband. God continued to challenge me to
surrender in other areas of my life. I have to surrender
every single day (sometimes multiple times a day). I rarely
get it right, but with God's grace I keep trying.

God started to address my thought life. My therapist
would say, "Does it meet the Philippians 4:8 rule?" I
know Philippians 4:8, but what the heck did she mean?
How do I deal with changing my thoughts and how I
think? (Didn't I tell you that God cares about every detail
of our lives?) He put Joyce Meyer's *Battlefield of the Mind*
in my IG feed. Unbelievable! How did I not know before

that God's word could help me with my thoughts? All these things had to happen. Trust the process and the timing. Through Joyce Meyer's book, the Holy Spirit showed me that I could control my thought life. I was not defenseless against my thoughts.

In Matthew 22:37-38, Jesus tells the disciples that the greatest command is that believers shall love the Lord their God with all their heart, with all their soul, and with all your mind. The whole person was represented by the heart, soul, and mind together. Therefore, believers should love God with absolute love and devotion.

God was strategically working on me so that I could follow His command. My Father worked intimately and intentionally with me so that I could walk in His greatest command. He healed my heart so that I could freely give it to Him. God was transforming my soul, and He taught me how to control my thoughts so that I could think on Him. Do you see that? Ordinary me and ordinary you— He wants us to follow His greatest and foremost commandment. He does not just give the command for us to fend for ourselves. He teaches me how to obey it, and He will teach you too.

We have to surrender daily to the greatest and foremost commandment. That's why I don't think this is about me or you fighting for our marriages. It puts too much focus and work on us. I don't know all the answers because I am still in the middle of my journey. What I am writing and what you are reading is part of my faith walk. I have to trust God's process and timing, just like you. I don't know if I will have a grand reveal that my marriage has been resurrected when God finishes giving me the words to write this book. Whatever God does will be what's best for me. I love the sweetness of surrender.

Surrendered spouses walk together during God's restoration forward. My husband is not walking with me, but God is. And I trust Him.

Restoration Forward

Where are you in your surrendering process to God? Choose one thing that you will completely surrender to God. What things do you find yourself surrendering several times a day? Is your "Fabulous Four" holding you accountable?

_____

_____

_____

_____

_____

_____

_____

_____

_____

_____

_____

_____

Chapter Five

Remove the Idol

DURING Lent of 2023, I decided to give up coffee (the only real food/drink sacrifice I can make) and add reading Priscilla Shirer's *Elijah* study to my devotional time. Shirer came out of the gate by committing to God's process. At that time, I was already tired of hearing the words "God's process" and "God's timing." Today, I have learned that there is no other viable process outside the one God has. Sure, we can live life on our own terms and things may seem okay, but they won't be because no replacement for God's process will get us to God's results. In *Elijah*, Shirer posed a defining question: Are you willing to do what Elijah did to get what Elijah got? The question was defining for me because I wanted to experience a kingdom marriage with my husband. But was I willing to allow God to do whatever it took *to* and *through* me? God started to perform painful outpatient surgery on me almost every day. I asked Him to purify my heart (and boy, did He do just that). *Could I handle "whatever"?* I was learning God more, and I knew whatever could mean WHATEVER.

I could not answer the question Shirer posed immediately. On one particular day of my study, God opened my eyes and ears to the praise and worship songs I enthusiastically listened to and sang. I went through my Maverick City playlist and asked if I really meant what I sang. *Do I demonstrate the spiritual declaration of the songs? Do I even try?* I cannot sing gospel music like I sing secular music. Singing gospel music is about my expression to God; it's about Him. No, I am not a praise and worship leader. I do know that songs that use God's word are an opportunity for me to speak God's language to Him.

I became hypersensitive to how well I could tolerate anything the day presented. And . . . I did not score very well. How long would I allow the failure of my marriage to be on display through a public affair, waiting on God's process and timing to allow Him to get the glory He won't be denied? I did the only thing I knew how to do: I asked Jesus to help me. *Ok, God, please be gentle.*

I was embracing the *Elijah* study, enjoying my time with God, when something else happened. I discovered something about my husband's girlfriend that I thought was a bit risqué and over the top. I thought, *Surely, he was unaware.* I shared the news with my husband, but I got nothing. I became completely out of control. (Yeah, remember, my support team had lovingly identified that for me.) Nope, I was not going to activate the strategies I had learned. Nope, no deep breaths. Nope, no using the tools in the toolbox. Nope, no listening to Scriptures. I once said, "I wish I could lay on Jesus' chest." It was suggested that I lie down and just listen to His word. No, ma'am, not on this particular day.

After I shared the news with my husband, I was set on taking twenty steps backward. I had not checked his girlfriend's IG before, but that day seemed like the perfect day to do it. *I may as well go all out on my downward spiral*, I thought. *Much of his girlfriend's information is public anyway, so what the heck?* I clicked on a video on her IG. It was on a date that was a special day for my family, and her family was singing in the clip. I could clearly hear my husband's voice in the background, so what did I do? I commented, "Is that my husband's voice in the background?" (Not done yet.) I went to a picture of her and a young man from the activity I thought was risqué, and I wrote, "What about my husband?" (Not done yet.) On a full fledge downward spiral, I went to a Valentine's Day picture and wrote, "Who got my husband's ticket?" My husband had taken me to the same concert where she was on Valentine's Day (that is a drama-filled sidebar that adds no spiritual value to my testimony). The spiral plane was starting to land, and I ended with commenting on a picture by saying, "You are a beautiful woman. You date younger men and married men. You are living your best life." (I know, not my finest moment but a true one.)

Regardless of how I felt, I was wrong. I was certainly convicted of my behavior, but what happened the next day in my *Elijah* Bible study was amazing. For months, Donna had been repeatedly saying to me, "Take your husband off the top shelf. God has to hold that space." I heard her, but I didn't. Then, her words became crystal clear. A section in the *Elijah* study talked about how God prepares believers for the assignment He has for them during a time of separation. I got it! I had become more mature and refined. Things like this were not supposed to flip me upside down. *Wasn't I ready for Mount Carmel? The place where God showed His power.* I was at the part of the *Elijah* study where the showdown took place at Mount Carmel.

As I read 1 Kings 18:26-29, I literally saw myself. I was jumping around, basically acting like a fool, and trying to get an idol to respond. That's exactly how I had behaved the day before when I was trolling my husband's girlfriend's IG (and many other days in my marriage) instead of calling on and relying on my God Almighty. I had put my husband in a position that belonged to God. My husband did not have the capacity to respond. I began to ask God to reveal anyone or anything that was out of alignment. He did. It may be good to ask God to do the same for you. (And yes, I still had to muster the strength to pray for my husband's girlfriend.)

With the help of the Holy Spirit, my spirals have become shorter and *almost* nonexistent. When I had a situation to discuss with Donna or Deneka, I would start my text to Deneka and Donna with "I am not spiraling." I finished reading *Battlefield of the Mind* and completed the *Elijah* study during Lent, and I am thankful for the transformation.

Surrendered spouses walk together during God's restoration forward. My husband is not walking with me, but God is. And I trust Him.

Restoration Forward

Who or what are the idols in your life? What is your greatest obstacle to removing them? What are some strategies to keep your idols off the top shelf?

_____

_____

_____

_____

_____

_____

_____

_____

_____

Remove the Idol

_____

_____

_____

_____

_____

_____

_____

_____

_____

_____

_____

_____

For Worse

Chapter Six

Forgiveness Complete

AS the Holy Spirit helped me remove my husband from being an idol in my life, God's word continued to hammer me about His love for me—His grace, mercy, and compassion. As God refined me, He convicted me of things I had done during my marriage up until the point when I'm writing this book. I agreed with God, expressed godly sorrow, repented, and sought to turn from those destructive thoughts and behaviors. Here is the problem with my husband being an idol: We did not communicate often. When we did, we both took a stroll down the past (much of which had become distorted and was purely a toxic means of reliving the hurt). However, I allowed my husband to continue to hold me to things I had asked for forgiveness from him and God. It was as if my husband made me feel I had to do more.

One day after a draining toxic discourse with my husband, I went back to God to repent. I said, "God, show me what I need to repent for in my marriage. My husband seems to be so hurt and angry. What do I need to do?"

God said to me, "Whose voice are you going to listen to? Mine or your husband's? I convicted you as I needed to. You have been forgiven. Stop asking me what you did because I do not know what you are saying."

From that moment on, anytime my husband brought up something I had done, I told him that I had been forgiven for the action. I told my husband that he seemed to like reliving the pain points of our marriage. (Again, at this stage, much of what was being said was either false or distorted.) It seemed to infuriate my husband that I was living and functioning in the freedom of forgiveness—something I had never done before. Here's the challenge: It appeared that deciding to accept God's complete forgiveness moved me farther away from my husband instead of closer to him.

I do not understand God, but I do not have to. I just have to trust Him. The Holy Spirit's job is to convict us of sin. We are to respond to the conviction with a repentant heart, and God is faithful to forgive us. That does not mean that there may not be consequences that have to be faced, but we do not have to allow the enemy to have us continue to pick up the guilt and shame. Jesus died on the cross so that you and I could be forgiven. The Holy Spirit knows how to convict and transform. I have one job, and that is to cooperate with Him. Remember, this conviction and freedom through forgiveness was happening while God was working on my idolatry issue. It wasn't until I was aware that I had an idolatry problem and was willing to remove the idol that I could walk in complete forgiveness.

Surrendered spouses walk together during God's restoration forward. My husband is not walking with me, but God is. And I trust Him.

Restoration Forward

Is there something the enemy has deceived you into thinking that God will not forgive? Do you think you don't deserve God's forgiveness? Has the enemy fooled you into thinking there has to be more to do to be forgiven?

_____

_____

_____

_____

_____

_____

_____

_____

_____

_____

_____

_____

_____

_____

_____

_____

_____

_____

_____

_____

_____

_____

_____

_____

_____

_____

_____

_____

_____

_____

_____

_____

_____

_____

_____

_____

Forgiveness Complete

_____

_____

_____

_____

_____

_____

_____

_____

_____

_____

For Worse

Chapter Seven

Release from Shoulders

I mentioned in chapter one that there are different perspectives in every marriage, and my husband is entitled to his. Over the last decade and a half of our marriage, my husband blamed me for everything. Things big or small—past, present, or future—were somehow because of me, something about me, or due to something that was wrong with me. I was in a constant state of defense. I had to defend my faith, prayers, discipline, motives, thoughts, words, tone, feelings, emotions, decisions, relationships, dreams, ambition, intelligence, class, actions, inactions—everything. (Caution: This testimony does not address how I got to "for worse." It's about a God who can rescue us from our "for worse" position.) I shared an overview of the blame my husband put on me with you because I want you to know that I started to shoulder it. I allowed the complete weight of the state of my marriage to be put on my shoulders, and I began to literally crawl from the pressure.

During Lent of 2023, I began learning to use God's word to address my mind. I was walking through the life of Elijah the prophet and applying biblical truths to my life. (You had to see how God was working then.) When I removed my husband as an idol (mind you, I could not see that he was an idol before I began the study), God transitioned me to acknowledge that the Holy Spirit was fully capable of convicting me. He had, and God's plan for forgiveness was enough. I had to have the courage to accept that if God convicted and forgave me, it would be finished. I did not have to continue to be charged again for the same crimes nor accept charges that the Holy Spirit did not convict me of. I am in a relationship with the Spirit, and He is at work in me both to will and do His good pleasure. His discipline is enough. I am not subject to false charges.

My Father told me I was shouldering things He never meant for me to shoulder; He told me to stop. For example, early in our marriage, my husband and I were friends with the pastor and his wife at the church we had been attending at that time. My husband went out of town for the weekend and the pastor called and asked me to go to the movies with him. I was surprised, angry, and upset (I felt violated). I told the pastor that I would not go to the movies with him, that he was making me uncomfortable, and to never do that to me again. The pastor brushed my response off like he didn't mean anything by his request.

I did not tell my husband about the encounter with the pastor. I did not think I could tell my husband because he was sometimes quick-tempered. But the main reason I chose to remain silent was because I felt like my husband would not believe or protect me. I knew what protection looked like because my Dad made me feel safe, stable, and secure all of my life, regardless of the circumstance. My husband and the pastor were in the same fraternity, and I knew that men lied. I did not want to go up against the pastor of our church, who up until that point had been a good pastor and friend, without knowing I would have the full support of my husband. I did not want to defend myself to my husband. Plus, I felt I had handled the situation. Now I understand that, regardless of how I felt, I did not give my husband the opportunity to respond to what happened to me when it happened.

About ten years after the incident with my former pastor, my husband and I were having a conversation about what his fraternity brothers would and would not do. He made one comment about how his frat brothers would not try to step to another brother's woman. I said, "That's not true. Your frat brother asked me to go to the movies when we lived at 1209 and you were out of town." My husband was livid with me. He did not say, "I am sorry that happened to you", "I should have been home with you" or "Why didn't you tell me?" No, he asked,

"Why are you telling me now? You have had me around this man. You are so disrespectful." I tried to explain to my husband why I didn't tell him in the first place and how I handled the situation with the pastor all while my greatest fear was unfolding. I was the victim, but I was being blamed. My husband expressed that he was not sure if the only thing that happened was the pastor asking me to the movies. My husband surmised that something more must've happened, which was why I didn't tell him. I could not have stayed silent for so many years simply because I didn't feel safe in my marriage.

For the next fifteen years, every now and then, my husband brought up the incident and taunted me. He never addressed the inappropriate behavior toward me or the lack of protection I felt from him. No, he only talked about how he felt and suggested that more happened between me and our former pastor (his frat brother). Again, the very thing I feared kept happening. We eventually left the church. Here's the irony for you: Like I said, the pastor who was inappropriate toward me is my husband's fraternity brother, and the woman sleeping with my husband is my sorority sister. (You gotta love the brotherhood and sisterhood.)

In 2020, my husband and I were having a heated argument when he mentioned the same pastor's name to me. Out of anger and spite I responded, "The pastor had good d—k." My husband didn't see me as the victim in the situation where his frat brother (and pastor at the time) made an inappropriate pass at me. He didn't consider how I might not have felt safe to tell him what happened. He didn't think taunting me about the situation for fifteen years was abusive. However, my comment that "the pastor had good d—k" was what he chose to completely hold on to. For some reason, I felt like those were the words my husband wanted to hear. I also think he liked reliving that conversation to prove to himself that I must have done something wrong with our former pastor (his frat brother).

Honestly, I was completely wrong for the comment I made about the pastor. I was convicted and received forgiveness from God. Then, I apologized to my husband again and again. My husband has told me repeatedly how what I said was disrespectful, and I agree. I also know that there was a lot more to the story than "the pastor had good d—k." I had been forgiven and my Father told me to stop shouldering this. (What a relief.) I felt like I grew eight feet tall. I would not have received that message from God if He had not addressed the idols in my life and that conviction and forgiveness are complete in Him. Again, the challenge was that my husband did not see these things as God transforming me. My walk in God's freedom and my desire to trust Him for my marriage moved me farther from my husband rather than closer to him. I was continuing to learn that I did not have to understand God or like what He was doing, but I had to trust Him.

My husband brings up the "good d—k" comment every time we have an extended conversation. I have to continue to remind myself that I have been forgiven and do not have to shoulder the weight of his accusations or comments about me and my actions. Recently, my husband added to the narrative that I should be glad that he was a good guy because he knew guys who hurt their wives for saying something like that. (He never mentions the full story.) Is there ever a reason to hurt your wife?

I shared the entire story with a male friend of mine (who is also my husband's frat brother) to get some perspective. My friend responded, "You know what you said was f—ked up, right?" I agreed. Then, he laughed and said, "The reason old boy stepped to you was because he knew what your husband was doing. He [my former pastor] wasn't trying to disrespect you. He didn't respect your husband because he knew your husband didn't respect your marriage."

I could feel the tears welling up as my friend spoke. I angrily and defensively replied, "That's not true. I don't believe that. My husband was not cheating on me then."

My friend asked, "When you did tell your husband what happened, did he check old boy?"

I said, "Not that I know of."

"Well, there you go!"

My head began to spin. Although I wanted perspective, I did not know how to process this viewpoint that I'd never thought to consider. My friend could see how upset I was, and he apologized for possibly overstepping. Then, he ended the conversation by saying, "I am saying this to you as a man. What happened to you was not your fault, and how your husband handled it was some bulls—t. Your husband ain't that hurt. He's been bringing it up all these years because he knows it hurts you."

Surrendered spouses walk together during God's restoration forward. My husband is not walking with me, but God is. And I trust Him.

Restoration Forward

Are you a victim of something yet the enemy keeps bringing false charges against you? Are you taking punches that God never intended for you to bear? Is there a voice of intimidation that wants you bound in guilt and shame?

_____

_____

_____

_____

_____

_____

_____

_____

_____

_____

_____

_____

_____

Release from Shoulders

_____

_____

_____

_____

_____

For Worse

Chapter Eight

Ain't It—God's Standard

ONE of the things Deneka warned me about was my husband returning and it not being God's time. She said, "Marlissa, be on alert." She knew how God had been working in me, so the enemy would be on the prowl to deceive me and hinder my trust in God. Donna, Deneka, and I discussed that when God does new things, you cannot base them on past experiences. Through God's word, prayer, and godly counsel, I understood that when God ordained my husband's return, it would consist of three things:

1. My husband would demonstrate godly sorrow for our past and present circumstances. (My husband continued to

blame me for our failed marriage, proclaiming that I was a terrible wife and ran him away. He also said that, although he was having sex with his girlfriend, it was not adultery or sinful; God had given him peace about it.)

2.   My husband would initiate the renewal of our vows.

3.   My husband's girlfriend would be transformed (receiving God's good plan and purpose for her life).

A couple of days before Easter of 2023, after not talking to my husband for several weeks leading to this point, he said he loved me and was committed to our marriage. He wanted me to stop the divorce process (which started in September 2022). *What?! You heard me, God!* This had been one of the most transformational fasting seasons I had ever had. I said, "God, You did it!" I was praising God as if Jesus had returned.

Even though I was excited that my husband no longer wanted the divorce, something didn't feel right. I knew what God told me to look for, and I did not see any of it. I contacted my attorney to stop the divorce. I began to pray for my husband's girlfriend (who had become his ex-girlfriend at this point) to be made whole and receive the good thing God had for her. I prayed that she was satisfied and content that God's good thing wasn't my husband. Still, something didn't feel right. I sent an urgent text to Donna and Deneka: "God did it! My husband said he loves me and is committed to our marriage." Donna and Deneka sent back "praise God" responses, but that was it. They didn't talk about partying like it was 1999 (the response I expected). I thought they both must have been busy.

What Deneka and Donna knew (and I realized shortly after) was that I was not ready for my husband's return. God had done much work in me, but there was more work to do to prepare me for my husband's return. How I was moving was confirmation of that because I was not surrendering to God daily or seeking His direction. I still did not completely trust God with my marriage.

We started to do what was normal for us, moving full speed ahead (remember Ezekiel and the bones with flesh and sinews but no life). My husband told me he wanted us to buy a condo in Chicago for the summer. He had been in Chicago the previous weekend looking at properties. He was about to start facilitating Henry Blackaby's *Experiencing God* Bible study at church, so I decided to start the study too. I thought, *Yes! Finally, spiritual intimacy with my husband. Surely this study would guide us to the work God would have us join Him in.* Unfortunately, my happiness about the things I thought God was doing to restore my marriage was short-lived. All of my thoughts and emotions were conflicted. You know, when your head and heart are saying one thing, but your gut is saying another. Later that day, a friend told me that my husband's girlfriend (the woman I thought had become his ex) posted pictures of herself in Chicago the same weekend my husband told me he had gone to look at properties. *So, was the condo for me or her?*

I asked my husband, "Was your girlfriend with you in Chicago? Were you looking for the condo for the two of you?"

His first response was, "How do you know that?"

I said, "Someone who saw it on her IG told me."

He replied, "Yes, we were in Chicago together, but I told you I ended it. I was not looking for a condo with her."

I said three haunting words, "Okay, I trust you." I forged ahead.

It was so easy for me to trust my husband. Instead of trusting God, I needed my husband's voice to validate God's voice. If it did not, I would choose my husband's voice.

I had prepared for this day with my therapist on how to handle specific triggers. I knew this day was coming, but the reality was that since we had been living separate lives, we would have to re-enter each other's lives. How we conversed and interacted was not what God had shown me—not an inkling. But I forged ahead. I utilized strategies from my therapist and God's word, and the use of the strategies angered my husband. He was bothered that I had feelings and was trying to manage them healthily. This was not what God had shown me, but I forged ahead. I thought, *God is resurrecting my marriage*

on Easter Sunday! Way to add to the testimony, God!
Again, I did not see anything God had told or shown me
about how He would ordain my husband's return. But I
forged ahead. I wondered, *Why am I moving forward?*
While God had revealed many things to me (forgiveness,
lifting weight, idols), I had not had time to walk in those
things before exercising them with my husband. I did
what was second nature to me: I trusted my husband's
voice instead of God's voice.

Two weeks after finding out that my husband was in
Chicago with his girlfriend (I doubt she was ever his ex)
looking at condos, he told me that he was in love with this
woman. I was surprised. I thought, *God, what is
happening? I trust You. I am too valuable to God to share a
man, convince him to be with me if he doesn't want to be, or
wait while he decides.* I reflected on the past several
months of my husband's "I love you but can't live you"
moments where he did not want me to talk to him about
his girlfriend. I asked God several times about this in
prayer, talked with my therapist, and talked with Donna
and Deneka. Everyone shared in some form that I did not
have to dwell in my husband's darkness. It is always okay
to bring God's light into circumstances. I did not have to
assist him in compartmentalizing. Talking about his
girlfriend meant he had to take accountability for his
actions and decide to stop. *Wait, what he was doing was
not wrong but peaceful. At least, that's what he had told me.
This is so confusing.*

When I mentioned his girlfriend, my husband often
said that I was evil and always had to do things my way. I

told him that I wanted him to be happy. If he wanted to be committed to me and our marriage, I would do whatever it took; otherwise, he could do what he needed to do. And just like that, he was gone again. He did not tell me he was leaving. We did not communicate for a few days, then someone sent me a video from his girlfriend's IG with my husband's voice in the background. I texted him while he was at a church conference: "I hear you went back to your girlfriend."

After watching my husband choose to leave to go back to his girlfriend, I thought, *Okay, God, this was worse than the blindside.* (Or was it?) Mind you, God did not tell me to do whatever it took for my marriage. God said that when He resurrected and restored my marriage, my husband would be surrendered and new. I would see the three items: My husband would show godly sorrow; he would initiate the renewal of our vows; and his girlfriend would be transformed. Oh, I was hot and hurt at God. I did not want to hear what Donna and Deneka had to say. I wanted to be mad at God. I needed to blame *somebody*, but I couldn't. God had told me clearly what to look for. At the end of the day, I knew that my husband's return did not meet God's standards.

My husband continued to facilitate the *Experiencing God* study for the church staff. Based on a few conversations with my husband and his actions, he thought the study seemed to convince him even more that his path with his girlfriend was God's plan for the two of them; it solidified his peace about his lifestyle.

(And to think, I was excited and thankful that my husband was facilitating the *Experiencing God* study.)

Surrendered spouses walk together during God's restoration forward. My husband is not walking with me, but God is. And I trust Him.

Restoration Forward

Are you so tired and eager for relief from dead spaces that you will accept a counterfeit? Has God given you glimpses of His presence and His movement? Will your "Fabulous Four" hold you accountable to God's standard? Is the real thing worth your wait?

_____

_____

_____

_____

_____

_____

_____

_____

_____

_____

_____

_____

_____

_____

_____

_____

_____

_____

_____

For Worse

Chapter Nine

Enough to Walk

WHAT *am I doing?* I thought. *My husband has not filed for divorce but is making no effort to reconcile.* My husband and I talk infrequently now, but when we do, it is a toxic rehash of the past with some "I still love you" thrown in here and there (from both of us). We bought the condo in Chicago together (because my husband needed to use our joint resources). He is still with his girlfriend.

I tell God I am okay if His answer for my marriage is "no." I continue to go before God for guidance, still hearing the same message. I am frustrated because I am experiencing so much (meeting new people, going to new places, and doing things I have never done before), but the elephant is still in the room. I do not see anything God said to me.

Some basic truths are starting to seem questionable, like adultery or sex outside of marriage being God's desire for us. We all sin and fall short of God's glory (Romans 3:23), but when did intentionally practicing sin—willful disobedience—bring peace? When did modeling Christlikeness stop being an important desire for believers? My husband and I do not talk often, but whenever we do, he always says he has peace about what he is doing. It seems the closer I grow to my Father in obedience, the farther away I move from my husband. I do not understand. How many times and ways can I say, "Thy will be done"? I do (and you do) what God calls us to: walk with and trust Him.

I have come to the end of what I believe the Holy Spirit has guided me to share about my "middle" on my marital journey. So far, I do not have a grandiose ending where my husband came home, surrendered, and became new. I have filed for divorce again, and he and his girlfriend are moving forward. I do not understand, but I know my intimate moments with God were real. His word is accurate, and His voice is authentic. I know that I choose God. God is my portion and enough for me: "Blessed be the God and Father of our Lord Jesus Christ, the Father of mercies and God of all comfort, who comforts us in all our affliction so that we will be able to comfort those who are in any affliction with the comfort with which we ourselves are comforted by God" (2 Corinthians 1:3-4).

As God has comforted me, I hope you have comfort in knowing that God loves you. He can heal your heart.

He can cause you to forget and unhear your pain. He is everything you need Him to be. God gave me two verses when He told me to write this book. I have to walk in Daniel 3:16–18, which says, "Shadrach, Meshach, and Abed-nego replied to the king, 'Nebuchadnezzar, we are not in need of an answer to give you concerning this matter. If it be *so*, our God whom we serve is able to rescue us from the furnace of blazing fire; and He will rescue us from your hand, O king. But *even* if *He does* not, let it be known to you, O king, that we are not going to serve your gods or worship the golden statue that you have set up.'"

I do not have to defend God or my trust in Him. If God does not do something for me, He still loves me. And I love Him. As I write, my marriage has not been restored forward, but I certainly have been. Psalm 73 sums up my testimony; the psalmist says that God is good to those who are pure in heart. During this marital journey, I have continually asked God to purify my heart. Initially, my heart was full of pain (hurt people, hurt people). Like the psalmist, I was envious that my husband was with another woman. I wanted to show my husband that I could date too, but I could not. The Holy spirit would not allow me to.

During this marital journey, my husband has maintained his position at his church without any discipleship or mentoring (although the leadership was made aware of his adultery). *I guess it is difficult to disciple someone who does not think they are doing anything wrong and claims they experience the peace of God about their sinful actions.* My husband teaches and counsels others. His relationship with his girlfriend seems to be flourishing. He has financial resources, travels, and has a condo in his beloved Chicago. He has healthy relationships with family and friends, and he has peace. On the surface, there seems to be no conviction, consequences, or repercussions; my husband is seemingly living his best life.

The psalmist describes the prosperity of those who go against God's commands (neither the psalmist nor I can figure it out). Then, the psalmist and I enter the presence of God and understand that God will not be mocked. He will handle my husband, His beloved son, however He wants. God is faithful to me! The best decision is choosing to be in the very presence of God. I pray that, in your "for worse" season, God will restore you, your spouse, and your marriage forward for your good and His glory.

Surrendered spouses walk together during God's restoration forward. My husband is not walking with me, but God is. And I trust Him.

Restoration Forward

Are you writing your conclusions because of what you see? Have you become a god by telling God what parts of His plan and purpose He can abort? Have time and circumstances made you want to try to explain your faith?

_____

_____

_____

_____

_____

_____

_____

_____

_____

_____

_____

_____

_____

_____

_____

_____

_____

_____

_____

_____

_____

_____

_____

_____
_____
_____
_____
_____
_____
_____
_____
_____
_____
_____
_____
_____
_____
_____
_____
_____
_____
_____
_____
_____
_____
_____
_____

Chapter Ten

About the Last Chapter

SIS, remember, this testimony is being given in real time. What had happened was that I became consumed with what I saw. I do not know how many ways I can live worse than yesterday, but somehow, I manage to find a way. Based on what I saw, I concluded that the story was over. The divorce has been filed. My husband and his girlfriend are set for happily ever after. My time with God is unbelievable, and I accept that God's answer was that He was not going to restore my marriage before the divorce was filed. *Wouldn't that have been the admirable thing to do? Hadn't I been obedient? Hadn't I prayed God's will?* (Darn right! Check, check, and check.) I stopped writing. I told myself that God didn't do what I wanted or what He said, but I loved Him anyway. I get to shake off all this embarrassment—experienced while walking by faith—and find myself a tall, chocolate Mandingo.

After everything that had happened, I found myself questioning God's will. I started toggling some things in my head. I prayed for God's will for me, my husband, and his girlfriend. I had been praying for a kingdom marriage as the Message translation describes in Ephesians 5:25-28, where my husband goes all out in love for me exactly as Christ did for the Church—a love marked by giving, not getting. Christ's love makes the Church whole. His words evoke her beauty. Everything He does and says is designed to bring the best out of her, dressing her in dazzling white silk, radiant with holiness. And this is how my husband ought to love me. I am to honor my husband. I prayed that for years. This didn't make sense.

I was starting to be more sensitive to how God was speaking to my concerns during my devotional time. I told Deneka I was not sure I could pray for God's will (because I did and look at what happened?). She encouraged me by saying, "Why did you stop writing? The story is not over." Later that day, I was conversing with Donna when she said, "The story is not over." I felt conflicted and thought, *I kind of want the story to end. I'm okay saying God didn't do it, or perhaps I heard wrong.* However, I couldn't get the vision and God's voice out of my head.

The next morning (day one), I read in my devotional book, *Jesus Calling*, how Jesus wants His children to pray to Him about everything. When we utilize the opportunity to pray about everything, we also have the privilege to leave the outcomes to Him. Hence, we never have to fear praying for God's will. God confirmed in my devotion that I could trust praying His will. That night, I said to Deneka, "It's okay if God isn't restoring my marriage, but I want some level of vindication."

The next morning (day two), a passage in my other devotional book by Joyce Meyer talked about how God gives us grace to keep our hearts clear of anger and resentment. We can trust God to be our vindicator. God confirmed in my devotion that I could trust Him to vindicate me.

I had coffee with a friend and shared that I was writing *For Worse*. She asked me the same question as Deneka and Donna: "Why did you stop writing?" During my devotional time the next day (day three), I heard in my *Abide* meditation verses from Ezekiel 37 highlighting God's ability to revive us (remember that Ezekiel 37 is one of the anchoring chapters of my testimony). God confirmed in my devotion that I could trust that He is present and powerful in dead spaces.

Then, I met with a minister friend (day 4), and he said, "Why did you stop writing; the story is not over. The just shall live by faith." *Oh, my goodness, I am so sick of hearing that,* I thought. *God, I do not want to keep writing this book, telling my story, and trusting You! I want to live life on my own terms.* Finally, I said, "Okay, God."

On the ride home from the meeting, God said, "Write how I am working, strengthening, and guiding you." I wrote this chapter you are reading as soon as I got home. We miss so much when we do not take the time to see God's movements. God gave me everything I needed to trust Him for another day. Ironically, I have been praying for God to increase my faith to a level that honors Him. It looks like that may be happening.

Let's review. I read three devotional books on three different days that are date-specific and all confirmed what I had been sensing in my spirit or a concern I was having. Praise be to my Father! God knew when each devotional was written or recorded that I would need to read or hear that message on that day. (Writing that sentence just made my faith grow stronger. When am I going to learn that God cares about every detail of my life?)

I tried to make my decision to operate by sight and not by faith as a spiritual one. My faith is strong enough to love God despite not getting what I was praying and trusting Him for. Oh, dear one, does it require more faith to hold to what God said despite what I see? My divorce is in progress. He (my husband) and she (his girlfriend) are they. Yes, I am experiencing God as I have never experienced Him before. I am evolving like I never thought I could, but why can't I give up? It's been too much, too long. Hmmm, this is God's story, so He gets to decide how He gets His glory. Me, my husband, and his girlfriend will come out of this looking more like Jesus.

Ok, beloved reader, what are we going to do? Let's decide together: we will walk by faith, not sight.

Restoration Forward

Has God given you something God-sized that can't be denied? Can you see how God is evolving and transforming you in your dead spaces? Has your relationship with God become more important than the "reward"? Have you experienced the sweetness of the process? Is Jesus the lover of your soul and enough for you?

_____

_____

_____

_____

_____

_____

_____

_____

_____

_____

_____

_____

_____

_____

_____

_____

_____

_____

Epilogue

What Now?

HAVE you ever been to a concert and the singer complained about her throat or announced a cough before she started singing? Or what about a magic show and the grand finale trick flopped? Well, ma'am, I am on the other side of the middle, and it ended in divorce. I defined this place as "the middle" at the beginning of this testimony. While writing this book, I have learned that I do not get to define the middle for God. The middle exists until God brings something to completion. I tried to put a human bookend (divorce) to God's sovereign plan and timing. I gave God a deadline to do what only He can do. It sounds prideful. It is not finished until God says it is. I don't get to tell God to abort. I trust God, but the outcome has always been up to Him. What if you and I approached everything like that? Complete surrender. Psalm 27:14 says that we wait for the Lord, we will be strengthened and encouraged, and then we wait some more. Notice that strength and encouragement are in the middle. I have waited for the Lord, He has strengthened and encouraged me in ways I could not have imagined. Consistent with His word, I have to wait some more.

I will walk gracefully during God's restoration forward by continuing to enjoy intimacy with my Father, surrendering daily, being obedient to His word, and joining Him as He speaks through my writing. I crave the things of God.

Continue to lean in, my beloved sister. The testimony does not end until God's will, plan, and purpose have been fulfilled. We will see each other on the other side. The just shall live by faith (Habakkuk 2:4). God is present and powerful in dead spaces.

Restoration Forward

What is God asking you to do next? Despite circumstances, how will you respond? Challenge: Look in your Bible to see how long Joseph (Genesis 37:2; 41:46), Abraham (Genesis 12:4 and 21:5), and Moses (Acts 7:20-31) waited. Then, look in the New Testament to see how long some people had been hurting before they were healed (you can start with Luke 8:43-48 and John 9:1-12 and 5:1-15).

What Now?

For Worse

Preface

Uncharted Territory

IT'S been several mornings since the divorce, and I wake up and am okay. I can't quite explain it, but I have left one space and moved to another. It's not for worse anymore; it is uncharted territory. People get divorced all the time and move on with their lives. That's not uncharted territory. See, I have been transitioning from worse to best. It's not best because I get to start life over. It is best because I have developed some practices in my life that have become non-negotiables for me. For example, I will never live a life where I can't have uninhibited time with my Father again. I will never go back to a life where all areas of my life are not surrendered to God. My, for worse, was not tied to my marriage; it was connected to my relationship with my Father. Likewise, my best isn't tied to the resurrection of a marriage; it is linked to my intimacy with my Father.

For me, praying without ceasing is no longer some arbitrary scripture reference that can't be practiced (1 Thessalonians 5:17). It's what I do now. Counting it all joy when I fall into various trials has meaning for me today (James 1:2-4). I have become a well-trained student who is excited to demonstrate my learning on exam day or the well-coached athlete not afraid to take the last shot at the buzzer. Apart from God, I can do nothing; now, I ask for His help with everything (John 15:5). I climb up on the altar every day and allow God to perform surgery on my heart (Romans 12:1-2). Some days, it's a quick procedure, and other days, I must stay overnight.

Sis, I am saying that I am doing life with my Father. That's uncharted territory for me, and quite frankly, it is for many believers. We don't do life with God. I have been a Christian most of my life. I have been a leader in various churches, and I was married to a minister. But today is the best time of my life because, for the first time in my life, I am walking hand in hand with my Father.

Now, what about what God said about my marriage? We can make this difficult or simple. Nothing about my best life is related to my ex-husband. My marriage was a conduit to get Marlissa to become who God created me to be. No other experience in my life, my children's health, my oldest brother's murder when I was a child, my other brother's struggle and recovery as a drug addict, my mother-in-law's murder, my niece's death in a car accident, my father's illness and death, the violation from the pastor, nor any other trauma I may have suppressed in my life was able to move me to total surrender to my Father. It's difficult if you want me to explain why God didn't do something. Wait, He did; He changed me. He didn't change me for my ex-husband; He changed me for what He wants me to do with Him (great answer, but not the answer to the question). Let me try again. It's difficult if you want me to explain why God did not or has not resurrected my marriage. I don't know. The answer is above my pay grade.

It's simple if I stick to God's word and His sovereignty. I know that for more than twenty-five years, I prayed according to God's word for me, my husband, and my marriage. I expressed love for my husband day in and day out by praying for His relationship with his Heavenly Father. I didn't pray for God to change my husband for me; I prayed that my husband would be transformed into the image of Christ (Romans 8:29). I loved my husband so much that the most important thing to me was for him to walk in his calling. Therefore, I prayed that he would be filled with the knowledge of God's will (Colossians 1:9-10). I prayed that my husband would love me like Christ loves the Church (Ephesians 5:25). I know that God's word says that I can have confidence in Him that if I ask anything according to His will that He hears me, and I have the thing that I petition Him for (1 John 5:15-15). I expect God's word to do what it says. That's on God, not me.

My ex-husband and I both made many mistakes in our marriage. We made each other an enemy instead of cleaving together against the enemy (Satan) whom Jesus had already defeated (Matthew 25:41). Still, it is God who works in us to will and to do His good pleasure (Philippians 2:13). My part in my love relationship with my Father is to obey and surrender (Matthew 16:24 and John 14:15,21). He has transformed me to where surrender is not only what I do, but it is also who I am. So, sis, I am not chasing my ex-husband, pining for him, or halting my life for him. I wake up every morning excited to join God in His plan and purpose for the day. God has control of my life, and in the fullness of time, He will do everything His word promises.

❋ ❋ ❋
About the Author

MARLISSA is a flawed, ordinary woman of God. *For Worse* is her first book. Marlissa lives in Peachtree City, Georgia and enjoys a good cup of coffee and walks at the lake. She lives a life full of God moments.

Marlissa has three adult daughters. She is passionate about walking with other women as they discover that God is present and powerful in the dead spaces of life.

Marlissa is pursuing an MDiv degree from Liberty University.